What do Animals SEE, HEAR, SMELL, and FEEL?

RANGER RICK BOOKS

PUBLISHED BY THE NATIONAL WILDLIFE FEDERATION

CONTENTS

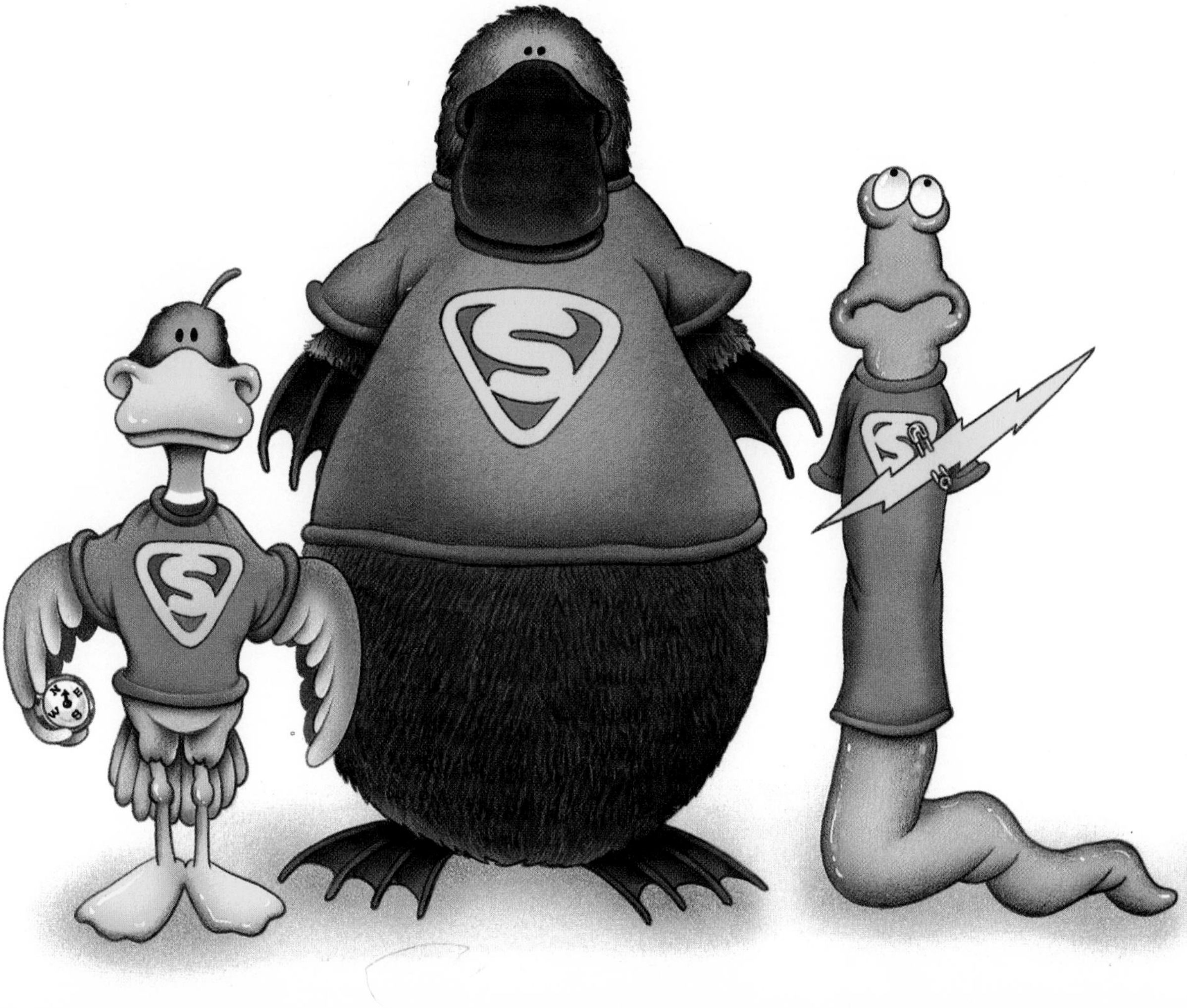

Did you know elephants can make sounds we can't hear? So can bats. Bees can see colors we can't see. And some snakes "see" their prey in the dark simply by detecting heat.

Because humans and animals don't share a common language, sometimes it is difficult to understand our animal friends. *What Do Animals See, Hear, Smell, and Feel?* answers many questions that can help us better understand them.

By understanding animals, we also learn to appreciate them. It is very important to appreciate the wonders of animals that share planet Earth with us. Animals of all kinds, from the smallest insect to the biggest whale, make up an important part of the world's web of life.

The National Wildlife Federation encourages young people to discover wildlife and learn about relationships between people and other animals. It offers special camps to bring you closer to nature and instill a desire to learn about wildlife.

NWF also has school education programs, so teachers can bring the importance of nature conservation into their classes.

And, the Federation is encouraging Congress to pass a law requiring schools to give students the opportunity to learn the importance of their natural world and how to protect it.

Let your imaginations take hold as you read about the vast and varied world of animals with special talents. You will discover that animals' senses are often superior to those of people. Birds can see colors of the rainbow we cannot. Owls can hear the tiniest rustle of leaves that would go undetected by the human ear. Dogs can pick up scents we can never smell.

Animals can teach people a lot about our own abilities. Have fun learning how a South American piranha finds its prey in murky jungle waters, and how an impala on Africa's plains helps its friends escape when a lion approaches.

And remember, while you may not be able to see everything a nocturnal animal does, by the time you finish this book you'll be able to see your animal friends much more clearly.

Jay D. Hair

JAY D. HAIR, PRESIDENT
NATIONAL WILDLIFE FEDERATION

LOOK! LOOK!

Take a good look around you. What do you see? Most people see a world filled with colors, with bright lights and dark shadows. In other words, we see all that there is to see—or do we?

We don't really measure an animal's vision with an eye chart. But we have learned that some animals live in a world that looks quite different from ours. We see a red, white, and blue flag. A cat sees a gray, white, and blue one. We see a rainbow that ranges from red to violet. A bee sees some of those colors plus ultraviolet, a shade beyond the rainbow that we find almost impossible to imagine. For some animals, seeing through fog or even making their own light is downright ordinary.

The Eyes Have It

To have vision means to be able to turn light into images of the world around us. Humans and animals of many kinds do this with their eyes and brains. When light enters the eyes, it sets off electrical signals that travel through nerves to the brain. The brain changes those signals into the pictures we see. Some creatures see pictures that are sharp and clear. Others see only fuzzy outlines. Some creatures see every color of the rainbow. Others see only black and white, like an old movie.

Even some creatures that don't have eyes or brains can tell the difference between light and dark. An amoeba is a tiny animal made of only one cell. Normally, it is visible only with a microscope. An amoeba doesn't have an eye, but its entire body —that is, the entire cell—is sensitive to light. In laboratory experiments, amoebas move away from bright lights.

The common earthworm doesn't have eyes, either, but it has light-sensitive cells, called *eyespots,* scattered over its entire skin. Since bright sunlight kills

Openings known as *pupils* control how much light enters an eye. In the dim depths of the sea, pupils in the eyes of the octopus (above) open into large rectangles, helping the octopus see better. In bright daylight, pupils in the eyes of the gecko (right) close to narrow slits, preventing the gecko from being blinded by the light.

A tarsier's eyes are so large they cannot move in their sockets. The animal has to turn its entire head when it wants to glance up, down, or to the side.

Hundreds of tiny lenses allow this horsefly to see equally clearly in all directions. But each eye would have to be at least three feet across to create a picture as sharp as that seen by humans.

them, earthworms must be able to tell the difference between light and darkness.

Most adult insects see with eyes made up of many six-sided parts, or facets. Each facet sends a signal to the insect's brain. Some ant eyes have only six facets. A housefly's eye has 4,000 facets, and a dragonfly's has about 28,000. That's enough to create a simple picture, but not a very clear one.

Scientists believe that most insects cannot see objects clearly more than two or three feet away. That is as far as they need to see, however, to look for food and to watch out for their enemies.

LOOKING ALL AROUND

Have you ever heard a teacher at the blackboard say, "Behave yourselves. I have eyes in the back of my head"? The teacher doesn't, of course, but some animals have eyes on more than one side of their body.

Jumping spiders have two very big front eyes and six smaller eyes—two in front and four on top of the head and slightly to the sides. The little eyes are called *secondary eyes,* and they can spot moving objects up to several inches away. Some of these secondary eyes have a built-in reflecting layer that helps the spiders spot objects in dim light.

The jumping spider (left) uses two small eyes in front to measure distance and two large eyes to make out details. The widely spaced eyes of the stalk-eyed fly (below) are a puzzle. Scientists do not know how such long stalks help this tropical insect.

Secondary eyes don't give the jumping spider a clear picture of what's moving, so it turns its body to give its front eyes a better look. These eyes are very well developed. They act like a pair of binoculars, giving the spider a good picture of objects up to about a foot away. If the object turns out to be a tasty insect or other prey, the spider uses the two small secondary eyes in front as a range finder to figure out how far to jump.

In the ocean, a scallop has dozens of tiny eyes that line the edge of its shell. These eyes don't see pictures, but they do spot the shadows that could mean an octopus or starfish or other enemy is getting close. Without legs, the scallop can't

The eye of a bigeye fish (above) bulges out from the animal's body, giving it a view to the front and back. A hermit crab (right) uses eyes on stalks to peek over obstacles on the ocean floor.

run. But by quickly opening and closing its shell, it squeezes out water and flutters away like an underwater butterfly.

SEEING UNDER WATER

Have you ever opened your eyes under water, maybe in the tub or in a swimming pool? Everything looked blurred, didn't it? That's because light behaves one way in air, and another way in water. People's eyes are built for looking through air, not water. Since fish live in water, their eyes are just the opposite. Fish eyes have a shape that sees best in water, not air. But one kind of fish has the best of both worlds. It has eyes that see clearly above and below the surface of water—at the same time. Scientists call the fish *Anableps*, a name that means "looking up." Many people call it the "four-eyed fish."

The fish named **Anableps** is also called the "four-eyed fish" because it can see down into the water and up into the air at the same time.

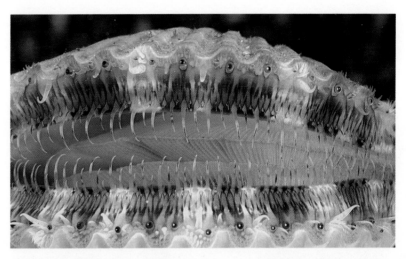

Anableps doesn't really have four eyes, but each of its two eyes has two pupils. And when this fish swims, one pupil points above the water and the other pupil points below. A special part of the eye keeps everything above water looking sharp and clear. Another part helps it focus under water.

As the fish cruises near the surface of a shallow stream, it scans the air for prey. It has no trouble popping up to snag a low-flying mosquito or other tasty insect. At the same time, it searches for small underwater creatures to eat. Every now and then it bobs its head to keep its eyes moist. And if a hungry bird comes into view, *Anableps* easily dives to safety.

One hundred or so blue eyes give the scallop a view in every direction. Even so, all it can make out are shadows; but that is enough to warn it when a star-fish or other enemy gets too close.

13

Where the Eyes Are

It's easy to look a monkey, a falcon, or even a tiger straight in the eye—at least in a zoo. Their eyes point forward, just as ours do. But just try staring down a rabbit or a frog. That's not too easy. Their eyes look out in different directions from ours.

If you look around at different animals, you'll see eyes pointing in many directions. Some point straight ahead, some point to the side, some even point straight up.

It takes two eyes looking forward at the same scene for a person—or an animal—to judge distance very well. Try closing one eye and reaching for something. It's a lot easier to do with both eyes open, isn't it?

Having two eyes looking forward to judge distance is im-

With its wrap-around vision, a rabbit in a park can take in the entire scene at right without moving its head. A person sitting in the same spot could see only the narrow area between the white lines.

portant for predators, animals that live by hunting other animals. A falcon diving at 150 miles per hour toward a smaller bird doesn't want to miss. Neither does a hungry tiger pouncing on a water buffalo.

Monkeys are not predators, but their eyes face forward the way a predator's eyes do. It's easy to see why. Monkeys need to judge the distance from limb to limb as they swing through the trees.

The animals that predators hunt—from rabbits and deer to small birds and mice—don't just stand around waiting to be eaten. They are on the alert for danger coming from almost every direction. And their eyes are in the best place to help them spot enemies.

With an eye on each side of its head, a rabbit can see in nearly every direction at once. That's why you can't get close to a wild rabbit. It sees you coming from any direction and runs away to safety.

Unfortunately, a rabbit can't see everything. Its eyes point so far to the sides that the rabbit has a blind spot right in front, close to its nose.

Whales have the same problem with blind spots in the front. Whalers knew this, so they always tried to approach the animals from dead ahead. Often the whales wouldn't know whalers were coming until it was too late to get away.

With two eyes pointing straight ahead, this lynx is able to judge distance accurately as it chases and pounces on rabbits and other prey.

Chameleons like the one at right normally sit in one spot and search for food by turning each eye in a different direction.

The American toad below uses its eyes to spot earthworms and other prey and sometimes even to hold slippery food in its mouth.

A chameleon is a strange-looking hunting lizard whose eyes can point in almost any direction. As the chameleon sits and waits for dinner, it can move one eye up while it moves the other one down. Or one eye can look to the side while the other one looks backward.

When an insect comes into view, the chameleon turns both eyes toward its prey to judge the distance. Then it's a quick SNAP! as the lizard's sticky, 5-inch-long tongue zaps out, snags the prey, and reels it in, all in less than a second.

The fish known as flounder start life like most other fish. A young flounder swims along with its body held straight up and down, one eye on the right side and the other on the left. But soon the flounder changes. Gradually, it begins swimming on its side and lying flat on sandy parts of the ocean floor. At the same time, one eye starts moving over to the other side of its body! Some kinds of flounders end up with both eyes on their right side, some kinds end up with both eyes on the left, and some can go either way.

When the change is complete, the flounder is able to lie flat on the ocean floor—with both eyes on its top side, looking up. This odd change is good for the flounder. Once it can lie flat, it can hide on the ocean floor while keeping a lookout for danger from above.

A frog's eyes stick out from its head and can see above, behind, to the front, and to the side—all at the same time. This allows the frog to look for flies and mosquitoes even as it keeps an eye out for birds and other enemies. Frogs can also lie hidden in a pond and poke their eyes above the surface to see what's going on.

Frogs do more with their eyes than just look. A frog trying to swallow a wiggly worm pulls its eyes down into its mouth. There they press tight against the worm so it can't get away.

Flatfish like flounder and this plaice start life swimming up-right, with one eye on each side of the head. But as a fish matures, the eyes slowly change position until at last both of them end up on the same side of its body.

The Night Has 1,000 Eyes

On a dark night, have you ever tried to find your way using only a candle for light? It's not easy, unless the candle is very, very bright. But if you had the vision of an owl, you wouldn't have any trouble at all. Your eyes would be so sensitive you could follow a trail lit up by a candle 1,000 feet away.

Owls, skunks, and other animals that are active at night need sensitive eyes to find their way around. People and many kinds of wildlife have eyes with two kinds of vision cells called *cones* and *rods*. These cells are located at the back of the eye on the inside. In bright light, cones detect colors as well as black and white and gray. Rods provide sharp vision in dim light—but they don't see colors at all. The eyes of nighttime creatures have more rods than cones. The animals see well at night, but they see the world in shades of gray. No animals, however, can see when there is no light at all.

You can see how well the rods in your own eyes work by looking at the stars on a clear night. First, stare at a dim star. Then look just to the side of the star. You'll see the star get suddenly brighter. The star doesn't really change, of course. By looking to the side you let the starlight fall on a part of your eye that has a lot of sensitive rods. These rods make the light look brighter.

Nighttime animals also have a special layer in the back of their eyes that acts as a mirror. If light passes through the eye without being detected by a rod, this layer reflects the light so the rods get a second chance. This layer, called the *tapetum*

Large eyes with pupils that open really wide help this saw-whet owl spot mice and other prey in dim light.

(tah-PEA-tum), makes the animals' eyes seem to shine in the dark. If you have a pet cat, you probably will have seen this shine. The eyes aren't making their own light, though. It's just the tapetum acting like a shiny mirror. The eyes' color comes from the rods and cones that the light passes through.

Tarsiers, which are tiny, nocturnal animals from Southeast Asia, have the largest eyes for their size of any mammal. A tarsier's eyes are so big that they cannot move in their sockets. Instead, the animal must turn its entire head to look around. Like an owl, a tarsier can twist its neck almost all the way around.

An opossum's eye isn't nearly as large as a tarsier's, but it has a feature that makes it excellent for seeing at night: a lens so large it almost fills the entire eye. By sitting close to the back of the eye, this lens creates the brightest image possible.

Opossums, cats, and other night creatures also move about some during the day—and that creates a problem for their eyes. Eyes especially sensitive to light can be damaged by bright sunlight. These animals' eyes have slit pupils, which can close even tighter than the round pupils in our eyes can to keep light out.

All these animals have night vision that puts human abilities

to shame. But people can make their eyes slightly more sensitive for seeing in dim light. Eating foods rich in vitamin A helps, a little bit. Eyes need vitamin A to work properly. During World War II, American pilots said that eating carrots helped them see better when they went on bombing raids at night. That was partly true, but the pilots were hiding the real reason for their success: a new, secret invention called *radar*.

Light reflected by its eyes gives this ocelot a ghostly appearance. A special reflecting layer in the eye lets light pass through the vision cells twice, improving the cat's ability to see at night. The green color comes from the vision cells.

Built-in Binoculars

To a rhinoceros, the world is mostly one big blur. It couldn't see an elephant at the other end of a football field. A human could see the elephant, but might have trouble identifying a mouse. A hawk, on the other hand, could spot the mouse a mile away. What makes all these animals see so differently? Mostly it is the inside of their eyes, where vision cells turn light into electrical signals to send to the brain.

The back of the inside of each human eye contains about 130 million vision cells, crammed into a space about one inch square. Together, both eyes hold as many cells as there are people in the United States.

In contrast, a rhinoceros's eye has far fewer vision cells.

As it searches the ground for prey, a hawk (above) uses telescopic eyes that make faraway objects appear large. The two pictures to the right show how a mouse would appear to a human (left photo) and to a hawk (right photo) if the hawk and the human were standing in the same place.

But a bird of prey, such as a hawk or eagle, has eight times as many vision cells as a human. These birds have some of the sharpest sight of any animal.

Vision cells are not spread out evenly in eyes. Many of the cells are concentrated in a round spot called the *fovea* (FOE-vee-uh). When we look at things, only what we see with this fovea is really sharp. The rest of what we see is blurred. To prove that, stare at one page of a book but try to read the words on the other page. You can't do it without moving your eyes to focus on the other page.

Some hunting animals, like the cheetah, have foveas shaped like wide, flat strips. These hunters can see everything on the horizon clearly without having to move their heads back and forth. That helps the hunter in its search for prey. Some birds, like ducks, swallows, and terns, have the same kind of flat foveas for seeing details along the horizon.

Birds of prey, too, have flat, wide foveas; but they also have two round foveas in each eye. These round foveas form little pits that act like binoculars. They make small, distant objects look larger and closer. Vultures may soar more than a mile above the earth as they look for food. From that distance, hu-

mans probably couldn't see the bird, but the vulture has no trouble spotting a dead rabbit or other animal on the ground.

Falconers, people who use trained falcons and other birds of prey for hunting, once used smaller birds to keep track of their high-flying pets. When they were turned loose, the hunting birds would fly too high for their masters to see. The falconers didn't want to lose their hunters, so they took along a smaller bird called a shrike, which they kept in a cage. The shrike has much better vision than people do, and it is deathly afraid of birds of prey. Because the shrike always turned its head to keep its enemy in sight, the falconer could tell where his pet was.

Light of a Different Color

Sunlight is made up of many different colors. You can see most of them when you look at a rainbow. Humans normally see a rainbow of red, orange, yellow, green, blue, indigo, and violet. But what do animals see? Do bulls really get excited when they see red? Does a honeybee busily buzzing from a yellow buttercup to a purple clover see any colors at all?

At one time, people thought that a bull's world was all black and white. They said that the bright red of a bullfighter's cape impressed only the audience. The bull was probably excited just by the motion when the bullfighter waved the cape. Now tests have shown that many mammals, including bulls, can see at least a few colors. Cats and dogs see colors about as well as a person who is color-blind to red and green.

Bees and most other insects see colors, too. But scientists aren't sure if insects see colors the way people do. Insect eyes may change the color of the

Blue is "in" to Australia's satin bowerbird. The male hopes to attract a mate by decorating his nest with feathers and flowers, even plastic scrap, anything as long as it's blue.

light so that a dragonfly zooms through a world where leaves are red and the sky is green.

Birds see most colors, but some Australian bowerbirds seem to prefer blue. Male satin bowerbirds collect anything colored blue, from flowers to ballpoint pens. These birds display the objects in their bowers, or stick houses, which they build to attract females.

Octopus color vision puzzles scientists. Most scientists think that octopuses are completely colorblind. Yet these amazing sea creatures often hide by changing the color of their skin to match the color of coral, sand, and rocks near them. The puzzle is, how does an octopus know what color to change into?

Some animals can see colors that people can't. One of these colors is called *ultraviolet.* Only insects, birds, and a few other creatures can see it.

Flowers often have patterns made up of ultraviolet colors in addition to the familiar reds, yellows, and blues. People cannot see the ultraviolet patterns, but they are like road signs showing insects the way to a plant's nectar and pollen. These road signs are very important to many plants, including apples, pumpkins, honeysuckle, onions, and clover. These plants need

insects to spread their pollen from male plants to female plants so they can reproduce. The insects are attracted by the patterns of ultraviolet colors. When the insects land on the flowers, pollen sticks to their bodies. Then, when they fly to other ultraviolet road signs, they spread the pollen accidentally when they land to feed on the other plants' nectar.

At the other end of the rainbow is another shade people cannot see. It is called *infrared.* Because their eyes are sensitive to infrared, South American piranhas can spot their prey in the brown-stained jungle rivers where they live. If people could see infrared, they would see the beams of burglar alarm sensors and television remote controls.

To a human, a daisy appears bright yellow with a small dark band (center photo). But to a honeybee (top), which sees ultraviolet light, the center of the flower stands out brightly (bottom photo), showing the bee the way to the nectar.

Real Eye-Catchers

Did the big eyes on these pages surprise you, maybe even scare you? They were supposed to. The creatures showing them off are trying to protect themselves by fooling their enemies. Animals that flash "eyes" like these aren't displaying their eyes at all. They are showing brightly colored skin, scales, or feathers. But because they look like eyes, they are called *eyespots*.

Some eyespots *attract* a predator's attention. Spots on a butterfly's wing seem to call out "Hey! My head's over here." But when a hungry bird pecks at the "eye" to make an easy kill, the butterfly usually gets away with only a few damaged scales. These eyespots draw the enemy's attention away from the animal's real head.

Other kinds of eyespots *repel* enemies. These spots stay hidden until the animal faces real danger. A hawk-moth, for example, often rests quietly on a tree trunk. But if a bird or other enemy gets too close, the moth suddenly spreads its bright wings, flashes its eyespots, and scares the other animal away.

At least one South American frog scares enemies in almost the same way. Frogs don't have wings, of course, but this frog has bright eyespots on its backside. When threatened, the frog simply turns bottoms up.

Eyespots aren't the only visual signals that drive predators away. Sometimes colorful patterns work. The bright reds, oranges, blues, and other colors of South America's arrow-poison frogs warn enemies that

Animals use many different visual signs to keep themselves safe from their enemies. The eyed silkmoth (above) and the *Automeris* butterfly larva (opposite) suddenly flash eyespots to scare away birds and other hungry predators. Bright colors on the arrow-poison frog (below) send a warning that predators learn to recognize. It says: "I am poisonous. Leave me alone!"

these creatures are poisonous. Birds and other animals soon learn to leave these frogs alone.

Although some bright colors and eyespots say "go away and leave me alone," others mean "hey, look me over!" Pea fowl are some of the most colorful advertisers in the bird world —and they send their message with eyespots. When the male, called a peacock, wants to impress a female that has entered his territory, he spreads and shakes his brightly spotted back feathers. If she responds, the peacock soon has another mate.

Sometimes the eye-catcher isn't another animal at all. Instead, it's a plant. For example, some orchids look like female bees or wasps. When a male bee or wasp tries to mate with one of the orchids by mistake,

At mating time, male birds often use bright colors to catch a female's eye. The greater prairie chicken (above) spreads out colorful feathers and inflates orange neck pouches, which also help amplify his mating call. The peacock (right) fans out his spotted back feathers and shakes them when a peahen comes near.

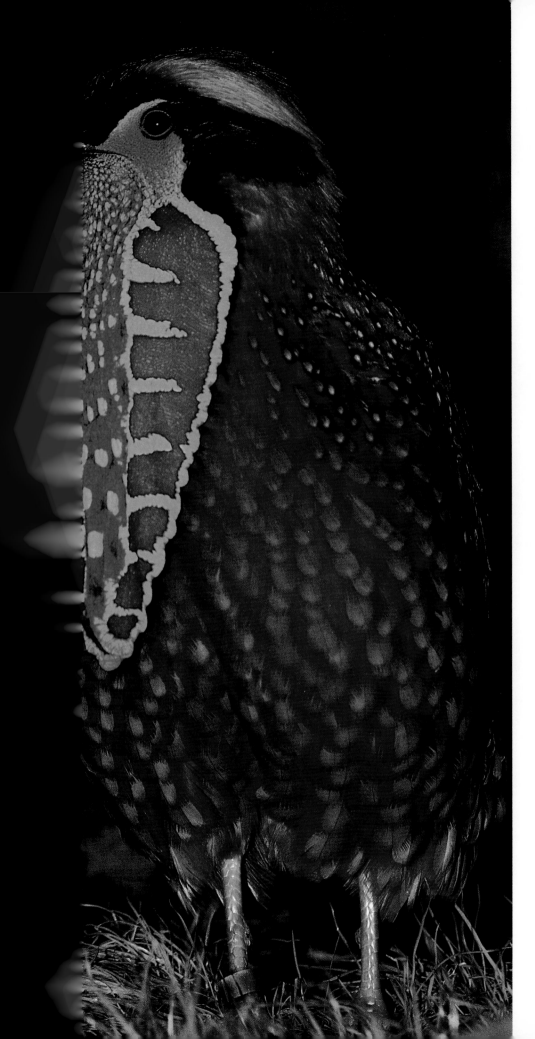

This male tragopan from eastern Asia seems to glow from head to toe when his courtship colors reach their peak. When showing off for a female, he appears even flashier by spreading his tail feathers and shaking his wings.

Because it looks like a female wasp, the European *Ophrys* orchid (top) attracts male wasps looking for mates. When a male lands on the plant (above), his hairy body picks up pollen that will fall off and pollinate the next orchid he lands on.

its pollen sticks to his body. Then as he goes from flower to flower looking for a real mate, the male wasp spreads the pollen that the orchids need to produce new plants.

For some creatures, it is not enough to be an eye-catcher by reflecting the sunlight. These creatures actually make their own light.

Scientists in deep-sea craft watch viperfish and anglerfish glowing in the ocean's dark abyss. Tourists in New Zealand visit caverns where glowworms make the ceilings shine like the Milky Way. And each spring, Japanese fishermen harvest tons of finger-sized "glow-in-the-dark"

squid. The fish and glowworms shine to attract prey. The squids' lights may scare enemies.

But you don't have to go far away to see creatures that make their own light. Just go outside on a warm July night. In most parts of the United States you'll see one of nature's prettiest summer displays: fireflies.

By turning their built-in lights off and on, male and female fireflies advertise for mates. Each species of firefly signals in a different way. Fireflies respond only to signals from others of the same species. That saves time when picking a mate from a group of different kinds of fireflies that look alike.

Fireflies (above) flash their built-in lights to attract mates. The glow of flashlight fish (left) attracts worms and other prey. A firefly makes its own light, but the glow of a flashlight fish comes from billions of tiny bacteria that live in pockets below the fish's eyes.

NOISES NOISES EVERYWHERE

Squeak. Rustle. Whoosh. Croak. A walk in the woods isn't always quiet and peaceful. A grasshopper's mating call may sound like an out-of-tune fiddle; and a chorus of bullfrogs sounds, well, like a chorus of bullfrogs. People and many animals depend on their ears to add to their information about the world.

Not all noises are obvious, though. Elephants "talk" in deep rumbles that people can only feel, not hear. And some bats send out high-pitched squeaks that even the most sensitive human ear ignores. That's probably just as well, however. If your ears could pick up every vibration, you'd probably get a headache from all the racket.

All Kinds of Ears

Ears are used for listening, most of the time. And it's easy to see where an animal's ears are, sometimes. The truth is, many animals' ears look strange to us, but even the oddest shape may help an animal survive.

BIG EARS, LITTLE EARS

Big ears may look funny, but they are super sound collectors. Just cup your hands around your ears and you'll sense how much better you can hear. Animals like foxes and bats use their large ears to help them catch prey and escape from enemies.

But big ears sometimes have other jobs. The ears of Africa's fennec fox and elephant help keep the animals from overheating. Because these ears are so large and thin, the blood vessels in them are close to the air. Even though the desert air is hot, it is cooler than the animal's blood. The blood in the ears loses heat to the air.

No one could miss seeing an elephant's big floppy ears, but do birds have ears? Do insects? How about frogs? You may never have noticed ears on these animals, but they all have them.

Birds don't have outer ears. They hear through small openings in their heads. These holes are easiest to see on baldheaded birds such as vultures. In other birds the holes are covered by feathers. The ear holes help keep a bird's body streamlined for flight. If it had bulky outer ears, they would get caught in the wind and make flight more difficult and slow.

Birds use their ears to hear the same sounds that people can hear, such as the chirping of other birds and the noises made by mice dashing through dry leaves. But birds can also hear sounds that a person could never hear. A bird high in the sky can hear the low sounds of shifting desert sands or the crash of ocean waves miles away.

Enormous ears sometimes do more than pick up sounds. The ears of Africa's elephant and fennec fox also serve as air conditioners. The thin flaps carry blood vessels close to the skin, where the warm blood loses heat to the cooler air.

eardrum

The ears of some animals are hard to find. A grasshopper (right, above) hears through thin eardrums on its abdomen. Birds, like this ostrich (above), have only small openings on the sides of their heads. These openings usually are hidden by feathers. A frog's ear (right) is also a small hole with no flap. But frog ears are covered with patches of skin that keep out water.

Such sounds are clues that help migrating birds find their way.

A frog's ears are located near the back of its head. They are small openings covered by a thin outer layer of skin, which keeps out water.

Many insects have tiny ears, although you won't find them where you might expect to. They are located in really strange places. A grasshopper's ears are on its abdomen. Crickets and katydids have ears on their legs.

Some insects have tiny hairs that function as ears by detecting sound vibrations. These "hearing hairs" are located below the eyes of a fruit fly, on the rear end of a cockroach, and on the antennas of a mosquito. Insects' ears and hearing hairs are often most sensitive to the noises made by their mates. But sounds also alert insects to approaching enemies and to possible prey.

One type of wasp has hearing cells on each of its six feet. During egg-laying season, this wasp stands on a tree trunk and listens for the faint crunch, crunch, crunch of the larvae of other insects munching on wood inside the tree. When it hears the faint sounds, it bores into the wood and lays eggs on the wormlike creatures. When the wasp's eggs hatch, the immature wasps eat the larvae.

You can't see a fish's ears because they're under its skin just behind its eyes. A fish's ears pick up underwater vibrations that pass right through its skin. Some of these vibrations are sounds made by other fish. Fish make noises by vibrating an internal organ or by rubbing fins together. They use these sounds to attract mates, warn other fish, or herd themselves into schools.

NO EARS AT ALL

As you've seen, lots of animals have ears. The list is long and includes fish, birds, some reptiles and amphibians, mammals, insects, shrimps, crabs, lobsters, and even barnacles. But some animals, such as worms, cater-

pillars, and many moths and butterflies, can't hear a thing. They depend on other senses, like smell, for avoiding enemies and for locating food and mates.

Snakes don't have ears either, although a snake can sense vibrations by putting its jaw against the ground. When a cobra sways to the music of a snake charmer, it is not following the beat of the music. Instead, it is tracking the gentle back-and-forth movements of the snake charmer.

Snakes are deaf, so how does a snake charmer perform his tricks? The snake appears to be keeping time with the music, but it really is moving to follow the charmer's swaying.

A deer (above), a jack rabbit (right), and many other animals have movable ears that can turn to follow noises coming from different directions. Having two ears helps the animals tell where their enemies are.

Two Ears Are Better Than One

People and most animals have *two* ears, and there's a good reason for this. Having two ears helps locate where a sound comes from.

How? It's partly a question of timing. A sound reaches the ears at slightly different times. This same noise also seems louder in one ear than in the other. The difference in a sound's arrival time and in its volume is enough to tell a person or an animal where a sound is coming from. A creature with only one ear wouldn't have this skill.

Have you ever seen the way a dog pricks up its ears and moves them around? Most people can't even wiggle their ears a tiny bit. But movable ears help many animals keep track of sounds coming from all around. A deer that couldn't wiggle its ears might run the wrong way, straight into a pack of coyotes.

A barn owl that couldn't track sounds would often go hungry. These owls use their eyes when they hunt at twilight. But on really dark nights, they rely on their ears to detect the rustling of leaves or grass made by scurrying mice and other prey.

The owl's ears are also at different heights, helping the owl pinpoint whether a sound comes from high in the trees or down on the forest floor. It's a lucky mouse that can escape from these expert ears!

The barn owl's heart-shaped face (top) may function like a reflector, making faint sounds louder. Excellent hearing helps the owl detect mice (above) and other prey on really dark nights.

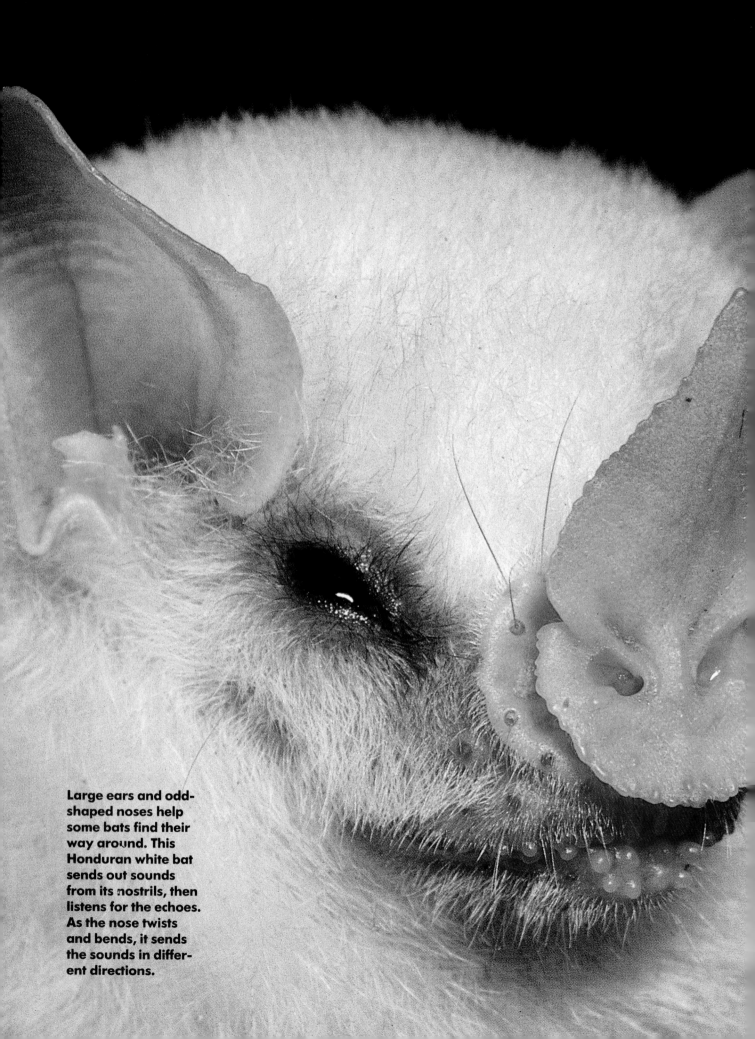

Large ears and odd-shaped noses help some bats find their way around. This Honduran white bat sends out sounds from its nostrils, then listens for the echoes. As the nose twists and bends, it sends the sounds in different directions.

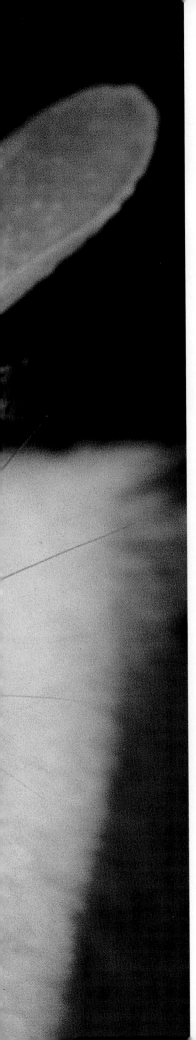

Seeing with Their Ears

"He's as blind as a bat." You've probably heard that expression. Well, here's a riddle: Why does a bat that is supposed to be blind have no trouble catching insects in midair?

This question puzzled scientists for centuries. Experiments showed that even though bats see quite well, many don't rely on their eyes to hunt. In fact, scientists found that a blindfolded bat could find its way through an obstacle course as easily as a bat with its eyes uncovered. Other experiments showed that bats couldn't navigate when their ears were plugged with wax. For years, no one could figure out how the bats were using their ears to "see" where they were going.

Then, in 1938, a young scientist named Donald Griffin solved the mystery. He used special equipment to prove that bats make sounds—sounds louder than traffic at a busy street corner. Why hadn't anyone ever noticed these bat cries before? Because the cries are too high-pitched for people to hear.

The bats in a colony could be screaming their heads off, but the woods would still sound quiet to us. It took equipment that is sensitive to high-pitched sounds to pick up the bats' noisy cries.

The bats' shrieks create sound waves that bounce off objects in their flight path, making an echo. By listening to the echoes, the bats can tell where the object is as well as its size, speed, and direction. Griffin found that some insect-eating bats detect prey smaller than a pinhead from three feet away.

This method of navigating by sound is called *echolocation,* or *sonar.* Not all bats find their food this way. Bats that eat fruit usually don't. But for insect-eating bats, echolocation is an effective way to find food to fill their stomachs. And for people, these hungry bats can mean fewer pesky bugs. A colony of 20 million Mexican free-tailed bats can eat more than 250,000 pounds of insects in one night. A single little brown bat can catch up to 150 mosquito-sized insects in 15 minutes.

Some bats use sonar to catch fish, too. Since bat sonar doesn't

Some bats use echoes to find prey. At right, a horseshoe bat homes in on a moth. A fishing bat (below) also sends out sound signals to find prey. As the fish move close to the surface of the water, they make ripples, and the bat's high-pitched calls bounce off them. Then the bat knows just where to swoop down and snare its prey.

penetrate the surface of the water, fishing bats find fish by listening for echoes bouncing off ripples on the water's surface.

One scientist observed pelicans helping bats find fish —though the pelicans were not helping on purpose. When the birds dived into the water, some of the fish jumped in panic, right into the path of the hungry bats.

Because its echo-making squeaks are so high-pitched, most animals can't hear the bat coming. But some moths *can* hear the calls—and dive to the ground to get away. Other moths make their own high-pitched squeaks. These sounds often confuse the bats and throw them off the track.

After scientists discovered echolocation in bats, they found that other animals also use sonar to help navigate and find food. Some cave-dwelling birds use echoes to find their way through the dark caves, even along the most narrow passages. Many animals that live in water also use sonar.

OCEAN HUNTERS

A dolphin uses echoes for locating fish. It sends out clicking sounds from the front of its head through a melon-shaped organ called, naturally, a *melon*. These clicks bounce off fish and other

objects. By listening to these echoes, a dolphin can tell the size, shape, speed, and location of objects around it.

Dolphins have fairly good eyesight, but they can't rely on their eyes in the murky seas. Studies show that even when blindfolded, dolphins have no trouble catching fish. But when their melon is blocked, they are almost helpless.

Dolphins make clicking noises that bounce off underwater objects, including fish. The dolphin uses these echoes to navigate and to find food in cloudy water.

Animal Talk

Animals don't speak the same languages that people do, but many creatures do use sounds to communicate.

MY ONE AND ONLY...

Many animals make sounds that serve as "love songs" to lure or identify mates. Several kinds of frogs may live on a single pond, and what a ruckus they can make when they all sing in one chorus! People may have a hard time figuring out who is singing what, but not the frogs. A frog can only mate with another frog of the same species. Females easily pick out males of their own species by the distinctive sounds the males make.

A female ruffed grouse comes running when she hears a sound like the beat of a drum. This drumming noise is the mating call that the male creates by rapidly beating his wings back and forth.

Male mosquitos' ears pick up only the vibrations of females' wingbeats. That's how males ready to mate pick out the females in a big crowd.

A male grasshopper "sings" by rubbing the thighs of his hind legs against his forewings. To a human, the sound may seem like noise. But to a female grasshopper, the screech is a lovely love song.

SOUND PROTECTION

Some animals use sounds to defend themselves. The rattle of a rattlesnake scares off animals that get too close. Small birds called bushtits burst into song when they see a hawk. The group singing confuses the hawk, which is then unable to pick out a single bushtit to attack. Scientists call these sounds a *confusion chorus.*

A male spadefoot toad fills his throat with air (right) so that he can croak loudly to tell the female frogs in the area that he is ready to mate (below).

Beating its wings so quickly that you almost can't see them, a male grouse makes a "drumming" noise to attract a mate. You might hear this sound in the woods in spring.

When certain frogs sing "croak, croak," it sounds like "yuk, yuk" to one of their enemies. These frogs don't taste good, and their enemy—the frog-eating bat—recognizes their distinctive croaking. To a bat, this frog's special croak means "don't eat me."

SENDING A WARNING

"Private property! Keep out!" That's what some animals mean when they growl, sing, or roar. Animals both large and small use sound to guard their homes and territories. They don't want other animals to compete with them for food and crowd them out. A wolf howls partly to warn other wolves to keep away from his territory. A hooting owl's hoots send a similar message to other owls. Flying to different parts of his territory and singing, a male red-winged blackbird lets other blackbirds know where the boundaries of his territory are. An alligator roars at intruders near its den, and a cricket gives a distinctive chirp near its burrow to drive away trespassers.

BABY BUSINESS

Like human youngsters, animal babies make sounds that let their parents know just how they feel. Some animal babies seem to make two types of sounds—frantic distress calls and softer

pleasure signals. A fawn may bleat its distress call if separated from its mother. The squawk of a baby bird tells its parents that it wants dinner—now!

Watchful mother birds warn their babies with specific instructions. Mother sandhill cranes use one kind of call to warn their babies to scatter from the nest and hide. A second kind of call says that the coast is clear and that the youngsters can return safely.

Female wood ducks use a special call to tell their babies that they are grown-up enough to leave the nest. A mother opossum makes a clicking sound when it's time for her youngsters to leave. If she didn't click at them, the young opossums would never venture out on their own.

A growling grizzly bear (left) warns off all intruders, large and small. A howling wolf (above) may be sending a message to others in his pack. Or, he may be telling other wolf packs to stay away from his hunting territory.

Like people, animals make sounds for many purposes. A marmot's scream of alarm (top) causes other marmots to run for cover. Baby birds cheep to let mom and dad know they're hungry (above).

A special call from a female goldfinch tells her chirping youngsters to be quiet so that an approaching enemy won't hear them. When scientists played a recording of this call, noisy baby goldfinches shut up at once.

LOOK OUT!

Sometimes, an animal's sounds warn of danger. A marmot whistles when a fox, eagle, or other predator is near. This whistle tells the other marmots to scramble back into the safety of their burrows.

Scientists watching California ground squirrels discovered that they use three different warning chirps. One kind means that the enemy is a hawk, another means it is a mammal, and a third means it is a rattlesnake. The squirrel's "snake" warning helped alert the scientists studying them that a rattlesnake was in the area!

Sometimes one animal's warning noises tell other kinds of animals in the area that danger is near. Gulls may notice an enemy sooner than nearby seals and sea lions do. When the birds sound the alarm to other birds, the larger animals automatically flee.

SOUND IN THE SEA

Land animals aren't the only ones that communicate by sound. During World War II, people were surprised to learn just how "talkative" fish can be. To listen for German submarines that might be patrolling the coast, the U.S. Navy put underwater microphones in Chesapeake Bay. One time, when the microphones picked up many suspicious noises, the Navy dropped depth charges to destroy whatever was in the water. They were surprised when the explosions turned up nothing but a lot of dead fish.

Most of the noises picked up by the microphone were made by fish called croakers, whose voices sound like a frog's croak. When millions of these fish get together during mating season, they make quite a racket.

Off the coast of California, the humming of male toadfishes keeps houseboat owners awake during mating season. Herrings make a chirping noise that helps draw the fish together to form a school. In fact, most fish make noise. They create sounds either by vibrating an internal organ called the *swim bladder* or by grinding their teeth together.

Shrimp also get into the noise act. When a two-inch-long pistol shrimp gets hungry, it points its open claw at small fish. When a fish gets close, the shrimp snaps the claw shut with a Bang! The noise stuns the fish, and the shrimp snags its dinner. The noise is so loud it has shattered the glass jars scientists use to hold the shrimp.

Some ocean "singers" have starred on their own record album, "Songs of the Humpback Whale." The 35-ton male humpback sings for 10 to 15 minutes at a time when it's in its winter breeding area. These sounds may serve to attract females to mate. Another whale—the white whale, or beluga—was named the "sea canary" by arctic whalers because of its noisy chirps, whistles, and trills.

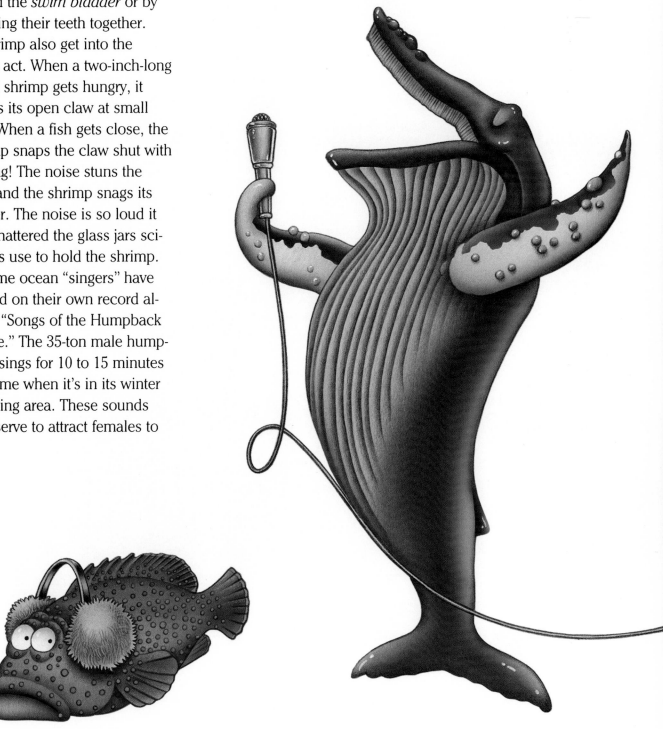

THE NOSE KNOWS

It's as plain as the nose on your face. All animals can smell—or can they? Super snouts on elephants and anteaters look perfect for sniffing. But what about animals that don't seem to have noses? Can a jellyfish sniff? Have you ever seen a butterfly with its nose in the air? Does a whale ever think something smells fishy?

No, not all of these animals can detect odors. Though whales live in the ocean, they breathe air, just as people do. They aren't built for getting oxygen or picking up odors from the water. If a whale tried to smell while under water, it would drown!

People have similar noses and smelling abilities. Animals have very different noses because they have different smelling needs. When you look at a person, you see right away where the nose is. But to find an animal's nose, you might have to look all over its body, even on its feet.

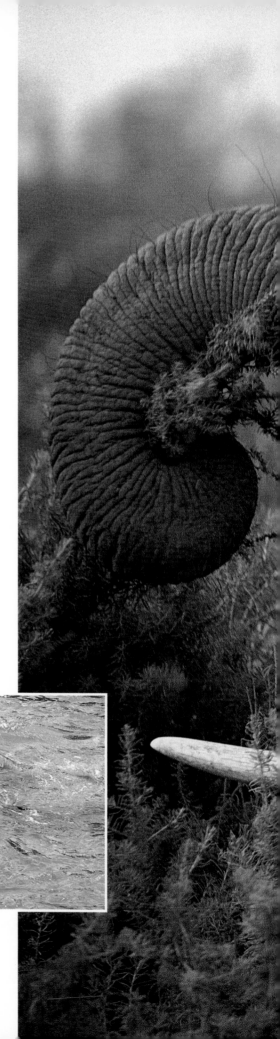

Notable Noses

Compared with the noses of some animals, yours leads a very dull life. Sure, you can smell food and flowers and poke your nose into other people's business. An elephant's nose is good for that and for other jobs as well. It sucks up and holds more than a gallon of water to spray on the animal's back. It picks up huge logs and holds thin blades of grass. And it can rise high in the air to sniff out predators and watering holes.

A giant anteater's sensitive nose helps it find anthills on South American grassy plains. When an anteater finds an ant colony, it rips the mound open with its strong front feet and claws. Then it thrusts its bony

How does an elephant cross a river that is way over its head? It walks on the bottom and pokes its trunk above the water like a snorkel!

An elephant's trunk is a 300-pound combination of nose and upper lip. The trunk does many jobs, from spraying water to sniffing odors to gathering leaves and other food.

For the coati (ko-AH-tee) (far left), a soft, flexible nose is good enough for sniffing out fruit in the trees where it lives. But giant ant-eaters (left) and lesser anteaters (be-low) need stiff, bony noses to poke into hard nests to find termites and ants.

nose into the dirt. Finally it pulls out the tasty ants with its long, sticky tongue.

The camel's nose has special channels that help it hold in moisture in the dry desert. When the wind picks up, the camel can close its nostrils to keep out blowing sand and dust.

Air-breathing animals that live in water can close their nostrils, too. They are trying to keep out water, though, not sand. Seal and whale noses—or blowholes, as whale noses are called—stay shut except when the animal needs to take a breath.

The male northern elephant seal's giant nose is just the thing for driving off other males during breeding season. The bigger his nose, the louder his bellow. Just the size of his nose helps scare his rivals.

If you were an octopus, you could nose around in all kinds of out-of-the-way places. Octopuses don't really have noses,

but the suckers spread out over their eight arms are sensitive to the chemicals that cause odors. When an octopus explores something with its arms, it feels and smells at the same time —probably the ultimate in scratch-n-sniff!

Sharks can pick up the smell of an injured, bleeding animal from a great distance, even though the creature's blood has been diluted by the ocean. A shark's nose is sensitive enough to detect one drop of blood in 25 gallons of water—that's about a bathtub full.

The male proboscis (pro-BOSS-iss) monkey earned his name from his large proboscis, or nose. His nose works as an amplifier, making his calls sound like the music of a cello. A male's nose is small and not especially noticeable until he is about seven years old. Then it starts drooping as it gets bigger and bigger. Female and young monkeys have small snub noses.

Why do animals have so many different kinds of noses? Because all animals, including humans, have different smelling needs. Each creature has evolved a sense of smell well suited to its lifestyle. To humans, the smelling feats of animals may seem like magic. But for the animals, having a keen sense of smell is just another way to get along in the world.

When a horn shark (above) goes hunting for food, the many folds on its odd-shaped nose (right) help it detect the faint smell of the shellfish it eats. The big nose on the proboscis monkey (far right) acts as an amplifier, making the animal's calls louder.

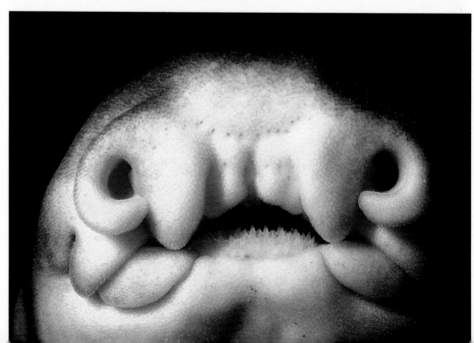

Alarming Odors

Smell is the best tool some creatures have for defending themselves or for warning others of danger. Skunks are probably the best-known of all the animal "stinkers." The blast of a skunk's nose-curling stench usually stops nosy dogs or hungry predators right in their tracks.

Some animals prefer to flee instead of fight. For example, African impalas give off alarm odors that signal danger to the rest of their herd. When an impala sees prowling lions, it leaps nearly ten feet into the air and kicks out behind it with its back legs. As it kicks, glands above its hooves release a spe-

By ignoring the skunk's raised tail, the hungry raccoons above risk getting a smelly, stinging surprise if the skunk sprays to protect itself. Impalas (right) give off a special odor when they are frightened. Glands on their high-kicking back legs release an alarm scent that warns other impalas to flee to safety.

cial scent that says "Run!" Soon all the impalas in the herd are leaping and kicking. All that jumping spreads the alarm and also confuses the lions.

The impala's special scent is called a *pheromone.* Pheromones are chemicals whose smells carry special signals to animals of the same species. An impala's alarm pheromone wouldn't mean the same thing to a rhinoceros.

Some insects, such as bees and wasps, also use smells to sound the alarm. In moments, a single bee can attract hundreds more to help defend the hive.

Minnows and some other fish give off alarm scents, too, warning their schools when danger threatens. But sadly for the minnow, it must be attacked before the scent is released.

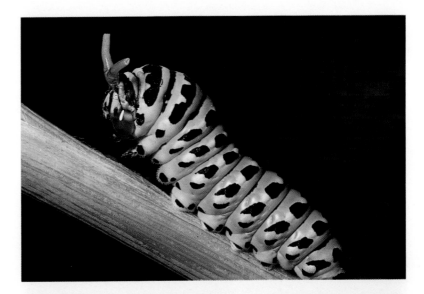

A bad-smelling scent given off by the anise swallowtail caterpillar (top) drives off birds and other enemies.

When a bee (above) fans air past droplets of an alarm scent on its abdomen, the smell spreads out and calls other bees home to protect the hive.

Hot on the Trail

Leaping up waterfalls and moving quickly over rocky river beds, migrating salmon follow faint scents that lead them to the streams where they were hatched.

From chasing down crooks to finding their meals, some animals let their noses lead the way. When you think of animals that follow a person's trail by smell, you probably first think of bloodhounds. These dogs, as well as coyotes and wolves, are excellent trackers for two reasons. First, their noses are really sensitive to smell. But the second reason is important, too. Odor molecules are heavy and tend to settle next to the ground, right where these animals' noses can pick them up.

Even some fish seem to use smell to follow invisible trails in the water. Salmon migration is one of the most amazing animal feats known. Salmon are born in freshwater and then, in their first year, swim to the ocean. Three or four years later, they leave the ocean and return to the streams where they were born. There they spawn and produce the next generation of salmon. Since the parents die after spawning, the new generation has no "old timers" to follow back to the home stream after their years in the ocean. How do they know where to return? After many experiments, scientists concluded that each stream has a different odor. The salmon probably navigate by the sun to get close to their native streams. But as they get nearer to the actual spot where they were hatched, the salmon follow the smell the rest of the way home.

Most birds rely on their eyes more than their noses for finding food. But turkey vultures are an exception. One scientist spent 25 years testing how well these meat-eating birds smell. First, he hid the carcasses of dead animals that he knew the vultures would eat. He made sure the carcasses were completely out of sight. Then, as he watched, turkey vultures flying overhead went right to the hidden snacks. They had to be following their noses.

This skill has made turkey vultures useful to people in an unexpected way. They are used to spot leaks in natural gas pipelines. The people repairing the leaks first put a "dead animal" odor into the gas line. Then they watch for turkey vultures gathering above the smelly leaks.

Most birds rely on their eyes to find food, but the turkey vulture (above) is an exception. It often finds its meals—dead animals—by smell. A hungry coyote (left) on the trail of a rabbit or deer or other animal easily sifts through all the smells on the ground to follow its prey's unique scent.

Marking the Spot

"NO TRESPASSING." When you see this sign, you know that the owner of the property doesn't want you poking around. Animals have their own way of telling each other what's off limits. They often leave messages by marking things with smelly oils.

Male bears rub up against trees to leave a scent that marks the edges of their territory. Un-less they are looking for a fight, other males go away when they detect another male's odor.

Animals also post ownership signs on other animals—and even on people. When your cat rubs up against you with its head and face, it's not just looking for affection. By rubbing its face glands against your leg, your cat leaves its own odor behind, telling other felines that you belong to it.

Mother seals often leave their pups for hours at a time and go out to sea to catch fish. The

When a bear rubs against a tree or post (far left), it may just be scratching, but it leaves behind a spe-cial scent that warns other bears to stay out of its territory. The cheetah (left) sends the same mes-sage by marking objects with its urine. The klipspringer (above), a kind of antelope, marks its territory by rubbing its smelly eye gland on a bush.

youngsters aren't lonely, though. Thousands of other seals keep them company. This is great for the pups; but finding her own youngster in the crowd could be tough for mom. You can't fool a mother's nose, though. The mother seal goes to the area where she left her pup and sniffs around until she zeros in on it.

Ants use odor to identify who belongs in the nest and who doesn't. An ant from another colony has a different smell, so intruders are easily spotted and driven away. A special "funeral"

Every sea lion pup has its own special odor, which mom sea lion follows when she looks for her family on a crowded beach.

The ground squirrels below may never have met, but one whiff of each other's scent tells them if they are related.

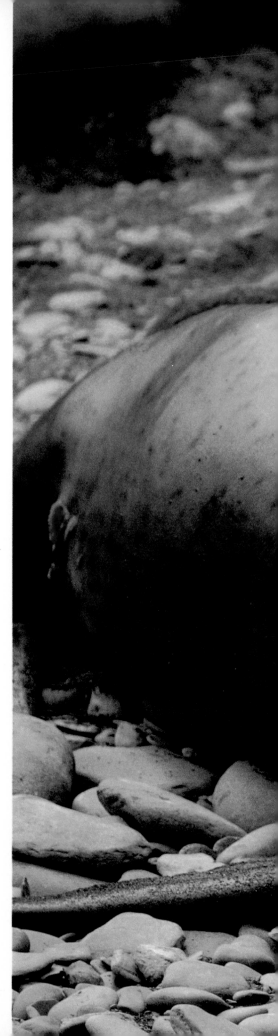

smell signals that an ant is dead and should be removed from the nest. When scientists put this odor on a healthy ant, other ants carried the marked ant to the burial grounds. It didn't matter how hard the marked ant struggled or how many times it returned to the nest. The other ants kept carting it away until the smell of death wore off.

Feathery antennas serve as a nose for this male polyphemus moth as it searches for the faint scent given off by a female ready to mate.

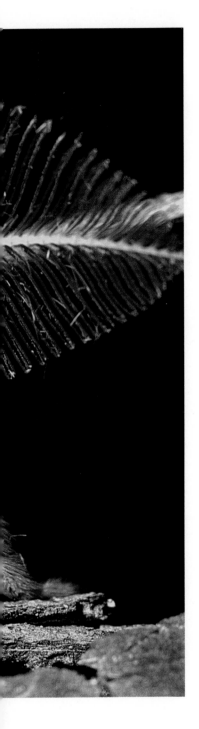

The Sweet Smell of Success

Animals often use smell to identify and attract mates. The right smell may bring a mate running. The wrong one leads to a quick brush-off.

For mating to be successful and produce offspring, the male and female usually must be the same species, or kind of creature. Many of the hundreds of different fruit fly species look a lot alike. How can the female tell if the male approaching her is Mr. Right? She often depends on smell. Suitors that don't smell exactly right are rejected.

The male giant silkworm moths use their large, feathery antennas, which are covered with sensitive, odor-gathering hairs, to find mates. Some parts of the antennas respond only to the odor of female silkworm moths. One kind of moth is so sensitive he can pick out a female up to seven miles away. That helps the male locate a mate in a world loaded with the smells of flowers, other animals, and even air pollution.

Things work differently in bee society. Each hive has only one queen, the female that mates and lays all the eggs. She is the "ruler" of the hive. Her presence keeps all the other bees, called workers and drones, peaceful and working. But how do the bees in a hive know that the queen is still around when there are thousands of workers and drones and no telephones? By pheromones, those special smelly chemicals that animals use to send odor messages.

The queen gives off a pheromone that is passed from tongue to tongue among the bees. This pheromone keeps everyone content. If the queen dies, the smell goes away and the workers and drones begin producing a new queen.

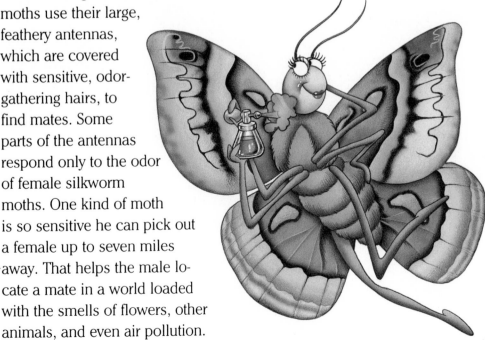

Tricks of the Tongue

Why are tongues in a chapter on noses? Because taste and smell are closely related. If you hold your nose while you eat, you can't smell, of course—and you can't taste your food very well, either. Taste and smell are *chemical* senses. Both the odors you smell and the flavors you taste come from the chemicals that make up everything around us, from flowers and perfume to milk and cookies.

To people, sugar is sweet and lemons are sour. But what do they taste like to a dog or a cat? We can only guess. What seems good or bad to a person may taste completely different to an animal. How else could a lizard with a keen sense of smell eat meat that has been rotting for days in the hot sun?

People, and some animals, sense tastes with taste buds. Each taste bud is made up of tiny taste cells, which last for about ten days before they give out from wear and tear. New taste cells constantly develop to replace the worn out ones.

Mammals generally have the most taste buds, and birds have the fewest. Don't feel sorry for the birds, though. Most birds get

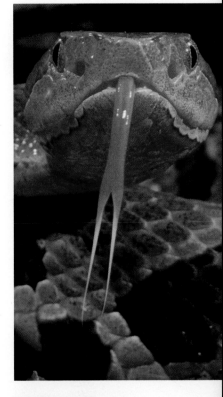

Smelling with your tongue? Snakes do it all the time. A snake's forked tongue picks up odor molecules in the air and carries them to a special sense organ in its mouth.

67

their meals in a hurry "on the wing." They don't sample food to find what tastes best.

Taste is important to catfish as they search for tiny creatures and plants to eat. Vision isn't much help in the murky waters where these fish live. Luckily, their bodies are covered with taste buds. Catfish can tell if something is good to eat just by swimming near it.

Insects don't have taste buds, but they do have special cells that detect tastes and odors. These cells are located on their mouthparts, their antennas, and even on their feet. For flies and bees and other insects, smelling and tasting are basically the same sense. Using taste cells on its feet, a butterfly can tell if a flower has the kind of nectar it needs just by landing on it.

Animals' tongues suit their needs. A built-in sunscreen protects the giraffe's tongue (top) from the fiery African sun. The chameleon's quick, sticky tongue is hard for an insect to escape (above). And a **black bear's tongue (right) is just right for pulling berries from bushes and for sweeping insects out of rotten logs.**

It's easy to see how the blue-tongued skink got its name. Some of these large Australian lizards try to scare their enemies by hissing and flashing their blue tongue and bright red mouth.

KEEPING IN
TOUCH

Octopuses, snakes, snails, and some other animals cannot hear. A few, such as blind cave shrimp, cannot see. But all creatures, from amoebas to blue whales, have this sense in common: touch. Some people call touch our most important sense. If we couldn't feel, we wouldn't know when something was hurting us.

It's surprising how much touch can tell us about the world. Blind people can read by using their sensitive fingertips to feel the raised dots that make up the Braille alphabet. Even with their eyes shut, most people can tell the difference between the feel of a fuzzy tennis ball and a bumpy golf ball.

Touching helps animals in many different ways. Using its hundreds of suckers as fingers, an octopus can pass objects up and down its arms. Tests show that an octopus can tell the difference between rough and smooth objects. The suckers also taste what they touch, telling the octopus what is good to eat and what isn't. To a dolphin courting another dolphin, the partner's soft touch is a signal for mating. And for a spider, the feel of a vibrating web means that something has been caught. That "something" could be dinner.

When touched gently
by an ant's antennas
(above), aphids give
off a sweet liquid
called *honeydew,*
which the ant eats.
The red milkweed
beetle's long anten-
nas (above, right)
may help it recognize
a mate by its shape
and smell.

Fantastic Feelers

Touch is important to all creatures, but it has one weakness: it requires physical contact. An animal has to be extremely close to be able to touch and feel something. Some creatures extend their reach with a built-in, natural solution: antennas.

Antennas are often called "feelers," but that's only part of the story. Antennas can feel, all right, but some animals also use theirs for smelling and tasting —senses that have nothing to do with touch. Antennas are so important that some insects have special combs on their mouths or legs for cleaning them.

Ants sometimes use their antennas to "milk" aphids. Aphids are tiny insects that live

The short hairs all over the body of a tarantula (left) are also feelers. They pick up vibrations and let the tarantula know when enemies —and prey—are getting near.

The Galapagos sea lion normally hunts for fish and other food by sight. But in cloudy waters, its whiskers help it detect the movement of its prey.

on the sap of plants. When an ant brushes its antenna against aphids, they give off drops of sugary liquid called honeydew. Some ants like honeydew so much they raise aphids in underground nests. The ants store aphid eggs over the winter and in the spring put the newly hatched aphids on plants to eat sap and make more honeydew.

The blow-fly uses its antennas to tell when the wind conditions are right for flying. By sensing how much the wind bends its antennas, the blow-fly knows how fast the wind is blowing. If the wind is faster than about six miles per hour, the insect stays put. A blow-fly can only fly about six miles per hour, so if it tried to move against a breeze faster than that, it would be blown backwards.

The honeybee has a wind-speed detector built into its antennas, too. This detector tells the bee how fast it is moving through the air. If wind gusts toss the bee around, tiny hairs on the bee's eyes measure each gust and tell the bee how much to turn to stay on course.

Tiny hairs on a tarantula—a *very* hairy spider—also act as "feelers." They pick up vibrations in the air and on the ground, acting almost like ears for the deaf creature. A tarantula uses its hairs for defense, too. When another animal threatens it, the tarantula drops off a bunch of hairs, which stick in its enemy's eyes and nose.

Some animals extend their touch with whiskers rather than antennas. Whiskers are especially useful for cats and other animals that hunt by night. In the dark, a cat with damaged whiskers has trouble killing its prey. A cat with perfect whiskers has no trouble at all. The whiskers help measure the victim's body and direct the cat to the most sensitive spot, the back of the neck. Otters and many other river, lake, and sea crea-

Both walruses (left) and catfish (above) use feelers to find food. Walruses poke their strong whiskers into the ocean floor to feel for clams, crabs, and worms. Catfish use their whiskers, known as *barbels,* to detect both the shape and smell of their prey.

Stinging cells in the tentacles of a jellyfish (far right) and a sea anemone (bottom) paralyze small fish and other prey. The sticky feathers of a sea lily (below) snag food particles floating in the water.

tures depend on whiskers to feel for food in cloudy waters.

Walruses have the largest whiskers of all. When the walrus feeds, it uses these sensitive bristles to find clams along the ocean floor. Some biologists claim the walrus can twist its strong, stiff whiskers around to scoop the clams into its mouth.

Fur seals' whiskers are also long and very sensitive. When a female seal wants to drive away a pushy male, she simply snaps at his whiskers and he takes off. Scientists often carry long poles for protection when they enter a seal colony. They use the poles to tickle the whiskers of any seals that threaten them.

Many fish have their own version of feelers, called *barbels*. Like many other antennas, barbels are especially sensitive to scent as well as touch. Barbels are the first thing some people notice in catfish. In some deep-sea creatures, the barbels are longer than the rest of the fish's body. Visitors to aquariums watch in wonder when the fish known as red mullet put their barbels into action. As they look for food, these fish twitch their barbels around rapidly and poke them into the sand, examining everything within reach.

The Portuguese man-of-war can't poke into nooks and crannies. But, like jellyfish, its long, drifting tentacles are sensitive to touch and they help it get food. Millions of stinger cells dot its tentacles, which drift for 30 feet or more below its puffy blue float. When something—even a human swimmer—brushes against the cells, tiny darts spring out and deliver a strong poison. If the victim is a small fish, the tentacles pull it close to the body of the man-of-war, where other cells digest it.

Feeling Your Way

Have you ever walked across a room in the dark and stubbed your toe? If you have, you know it hurts. The pain probably slowed you down for a little while. But chances are you forgot all about your sore toe in just a few minutes. However, if a wild animal were to stumble in the dark, the result could be deadly. That animal might get caught and end up as another creature's dinner.

Luckily, the sense of touch enables many animals to detect dangers before they run into them. Picture the desert jerboa, a mouse-sized rodent found in Africa and Asia. The jerboa jumps like a kangaroo as it dashes across the ground at night. One bump into an unseen rock or plant could trip the jerboa and send it crashing headfirst to the ground.

The star-nosed mole is almost completely blind, but it has little trouble finding worms and other food as it uses its sensitive nose to feel its way through its tunnels.

Even at full speed, the jerboa rarely misses a step. It twists almost magically at the last moment and avoids tripping or landing in a hole. How does it spot these problems when it's two inches off the ground and darkness prevents its seeing them? It depends on two whiskers, which are almost as long as its body, that drag the ground at all times. If the whiskers detect a rock, the jerboa swings its tail to one side or the other and changes course in midair.

Feelers help when creatures move slowly, too. A star-nosed mole is almost completely blind, but it has no trouble catching worms and insects or avoiding rocks as it burrows through the ground. It simply follows its nose. The mole's odd-shaped nose isn't built for smelling, though. It's really a sensitive feeler dotted with short hairs. Nerve endings at the base of the hairs make the nose sensitive to touch and also to the electricity generated by the prey's muscles.

According to an old saying, if a cat can get its head through a hole, it can get the rest of its body through. What this really means is that a cat measures the hole with its whiskers. If a small hole bends the whiskers too far back, the cat knows there's not enough room.

When some animals feel their way around, they measure what they're touching. A queen bee laying eggs measures each cell in the hive before putting an egg in it. Sensitive hairs on her abdomen tell her if the cell is small or large. If the cell is small, she puts in a fertilized egg. This egg becomes a worker bee, whose duty is to gather honey, take care of the hive, and raise young bees. But if the cell is large, the queen lays an unfertilized egg there. This egg becomes a drone. Drones are males whose main job is to mate with special female bees, which become new queens.

A star-nosed mole's "star" is covered with short hairs that detect rocks and worms and other objects in the mole's path. Scientists have recently learned that the mole's nose can detect the faint electricity given off by animals' muscles.

Caddisfly larvae also use their hairs as yardsticks. These insects measure the size of the nests that they build and carry around at all times. Their built-in rulers tell the larvae when to stop building. A larva whose hairs have been cut keeps on working until its nest is too big to move.

With its sensitive, sucker-covered arms, an octopus will pick up small objects and examine them by touch. Each sucker is a combination finger and tongue. It feels objects and tastes them at the same time.

Bee-hunting wasps feel their way to victory when they chase their prey. The wasp's stinger can't poke through the bee's tough body, but the bee has a tiny, soft spot where it is de-fenseless. When the wasp attacks, it uses its touch senses to find this spot. The wasp has to be quick or the bee will get away. Since its feeler is right by its stinger, the hunting wasp often has no problem zapping its prey to snare its dinner.

Some creatures use their sense of touch to help them take care of their young. Wolf spiders protect their round egg sacs by carrying them until the eggs hatch. The spiders' instinct is to pick up and protect anything that feels small and round. If the spider drops her egg case, she pokes around until she finds something that feels like it. Sometimes she ends up carrying empty snail shells, wads of paper, even rabbit droppings.

Hundreds of sensitive suction cups help an octopus (far left) hold, feel, and even taste objects.

Whenever a wolf spider (left) feels something round with its legs and mouthparts, it instinctively picks it up. That instinct helps the spider keep its round egg case safe in its care until the eggs hatch.

Touching Moments

With a steady tap, tap, tap, a young spoonbill tells its parent, "I'm hungry!" Mom and dad respond by coughing up partly digested food, which they push into the youngster's throat.

Snuggle, hug, and kiss—people often touch each other to show love and affection. Sometimes an animal's touch is also a sign of what people might call love. Among dolphins, one creature's soft nuzzling wakens the urge to mate in another. Some sala-

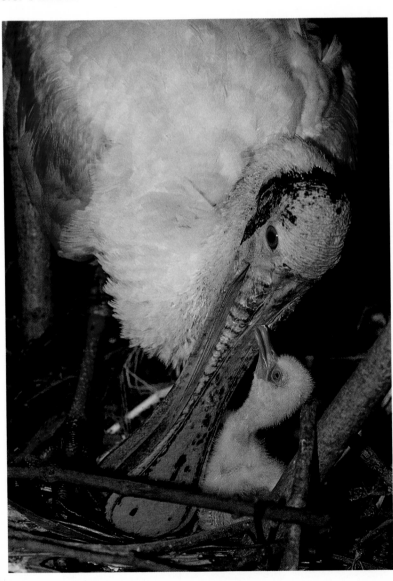

manders court by waving their tails and rubbing their noses together. And a male giraffe gets a female interested in him by rubbing his neck around hers— an activity called "necking."

At other times, an animal's soft touch has a more down-to-earth purpose. By tapping on its mother's beak, a baby spoonbill announces, "I'm hungry!" All it takes is this touch, and the mother opens her beak and coughs up her last meal for the baby bird to eat. A young herring gull begs for food in almost the same way. It pecks at a red spot on its parent's beak.

Monkeys in a group often groom each other, picking off pesky insects. Grooming keeps the monkeys clean, but it also serves another purpose. The touching helps the individual animals feel like they are part of the group.

By rubbing against each other, lions relieve tension that might lead to fighting. Lions live in groups called prides. Within a pride, female lions often rub heads as a peaceful greeting. A cub will also run to its mother and rub her to say hello. Lion mothers often lick their cubs. Like the monkeys' grooming, the licking does more than just clean the cub. It tells the baby lion that it is a welcome part of the family.

From poking to snuggling, many animals seem to enjoy each other's touch. When one monkey cleans another (above) or a lion cub leans against its mother (left), the touching makes each animal feel like part of a close-knit group.

Great Vibrations

Try putting your hand on a loud radio or on the dashboard of your car when the motor is running. You can probably feel it vibrating. This sensitivity is part of touch, too, and it helps many creatures survive.

When a spider's web shakes, the spider normally can tell if it has caught dinner, a mate, or a falling leaf. Waiting at the edge of its web, the spider picks up the web's vibrations through its legs. When an insect or other tiny creature gets stuck on the web and twists and turns trying to get away, it causes the web to vibrate. These vibrations are different from those caused by a leaf landing on the web or a suitor trying to get the spider's attention. When a

spider returns to its web after having been somewhere else for a while, it tugs on the web to see how it feels. It can tell if something is stuck there by the way the web shakes.

Male orb-weaving spiders send their courtship signals through the female's web. When the male touches her web, he starts vibrating his body. This vibration is different from the vibration caused by a stuck insect, and the female can tell the difference. This time she moves across the web ready to mate rather than pounce on dinner.

Sometimes even the youngest spiders know how to "read" vibrations. When a mother funnel spider builds her wide, flat web on the forest floor, she adds on a nursery for her young. When beetles or other prey get stuck, the mother comes out to attack. As she feeds on the captured animal, her body gives off soft vibrations. To the youngsters back in the nursery, this gentle shaking carries a special message: "Dinner's ready!"

Fish follow vibrations, too, and not always to find food or mates. Male Siamese fighting fish guard their young until they are old enough to survive on their own. As the young fish start to explore their world, the father

The female European garden spider (left) often waits at the center of her web, ready to attack anything that touches it. When a male garden spider plucks the web in a special way, however, she rushes to meet him (below). Usually the two mate, but sometimes the female kills and eats the male.

swims nearby and doesn't interfere. But if danger threatens, he starts shaking violently. The youngsters sense their father's vibrations and swim into his mouth. He then carries them back to the safety of their nest.

Vibrations mean danger to earthworms, too. Earthworms live underground; but so do moles, which eat earthworms. Whenever a mole burrows through the ground, the vibrations made by its tunneling send earthworms slithering out of the ground to safety. People going fishing sometimes try to imitate the mole's "sound" to catch worms for bait. The system is simple: push a stick into the ground, wiggle it around, and catch the worms when they poke out of the soil.

SUPER SENSES

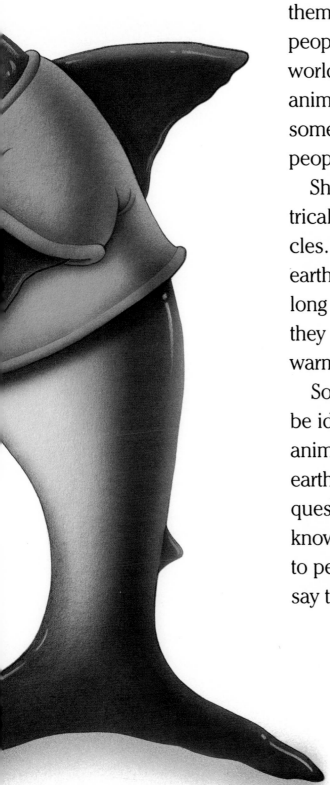

Look at things. Listen to them. Touch them. Smell them. Taste them. That's how people—and most animals—learn about the world around them. In many ways, some animals are better at this than people. But some creatures also rely on senses that people do not have.

Sharks, for example, home in on electrical signals given off by their prey's muscles. In bad weather, birds follow the earth's magnetic field as they migrate over long distances. Rattlesnakes strike when they "see" the heat given off by their warmblooded targets.

Sometimes animals use senses that can't be identified for sure. What makes some animals act in strange ways just before an earthquake hits? People have asked this question for hundreds of years. Until it's known for sure what enables some animals to perform amazing feats, maybe it's fair to say that they are using "super senses."

Natural Gifts

When it comes to "super senses," truth really is as strange as fiction. People in ancient Mesopotamia thought that ants could sense the approach of enemy warriors. Soldiers on guard would watch ants, and if the insects started fighting, the soldiers believed the enemy was getting near. That belief was just a superstition, but animals do have senses that may seem just as incredible.

SENSING ELECTRICITY

Platypuses, which live in Australia, can't see very well. Yet they have no problem finding prey hidden in the muddy bottoms of streams. How do they do it? No, it isn't magic. The muscles of all animals create tiny amounts of electricity when they move. The platypus has sensitive cells that detect this electricity. Every twitch, every heartbeat of nearby prey carries a clear message to the platypus: "Here I am!"

Sharks and rays also detect electricity, at least when their prey is no more than about three feet away. This helps them find creatures hiding in murky water or buried on the ocean floor.

South American knifefish give off electrical discharges so strong they act like radar. By bouncing off rocks and even other fish, these electrical "echoes" help the knifefish find their way through muddy water. Sometimes the fish examine strange objects by swimming backward and forward alongside the object while sending out discharges at a rapid pace.

Certain catfish and eels give off more electricity than any other animals. Ancient Egyptians called the Nile's electric catfish "he who releases many" because fishermen who were shocked by the eel would drop their catch. In the Middle Ages, people put electric catfish on their bodies to treat aches and pains.

South America's electric eels are much too powerful and dangerous to use this way. At eight feet long, a full-grown eel

Special sensors on the head of a shark, like the silvertip shark (below), help these creatures home in on the faint electricity given off by their prey's muscles.

weighs about 60 pounds—more than half of which is muscle for producing electricity. An average-sized electric eel can stun a horse in the water 20 feet away or kill anyone foolish enough to touch it.

Why don't these catfish and eels hurt themselves when they make electricity to stun their prey? That's a question scientists still have not answered.

FEELING THE HEAT

Mosquitoes are real pests, especially when the females buzz around your head looking for a place to land and bite. Have you ever wondered how they find

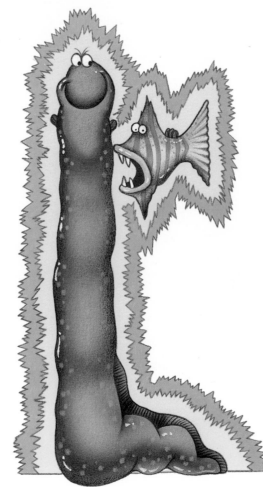

Electricity detectors on the bill of an Australian platypus (above) are sensitive enough to pick out small shrimp more than three feet away.

Latin America's electric eel (left) is a living battery. When it zaps the water with up to 500 volts of electricity, it drives away large enemies and stuns small prey.

you even in the dark? They follow several signs, including the moisture in your breath. But they also use a heat sense that leads them straight to their warm-blooded victims.

Female mosquitoes can sense temperature differences of less than $\frac{1}{250}$th of a degree F. That lets a hungry mosquito on the prowl pinpoint where it has the best chance of tapping into a vein of warm blood.

Vampire bats, which also feed on blood, use their heat sensitivity for the same purpose: getting a meal. By detecting the presence of warm blood vessels near the surface of their victim's skin, they home in on the best place to bite.

Latin American vampire bats live on the blood of cattle and other animals. These bats have heat sensors that tell where their warm-blooded victim's blood vessels lie closest to the surface of the skin.

The snakes known as pit vipers have some of the most accurate heat-sensing equipment in the animal world. This family includes the most common poisonous snakes in the United States: rattlesnakes, copperheads, and water moccasins.

A pit viper's pits are two small holes on the head just behind the nostrils. Each opening is a bit smaller than a pencil's eraser. About 150,000 heat-sensitive nerve cells inside each pit pick up the faint heat waves given off by warm bodies. By moving their heads from side to side, the snakes can "see" the size and shape of their prey even in the dark.

Heat sensors help snakes in the daytime, too. Some animals that the snakes hunt have colors that act as camouflage. Normally, these animals can hide by blending into the background. But when the pit viper points its heat sensors in their direction, they stand out clearly.

ANIMAL MAGNETISM

If you've ever used a compass, you know that the needle swings to point north. The needle is magnetic, and it moves to line up with a magnetic field that surrounds the earth. Birds, bees, and some other animals have a built-in compass that they use to tell direction. Their natural mag-

nets are tiny crystals of iron oxide, or magnetite, made from iron found in their food.

Bees normally rely on the sun for finding the way between their hive and food sources. But when scientists in Hawaii set up tests in which the bees couldn't see the sun, the bees found their way anyway. Did the bees really use a magnetic sense? To be sure, the scientists fastened tiny magnets to some of the bees. The bees' magnetite crystals pointed to the magnets instead of the earth's magnetic field. Tests then showed that the bees without the magnets had no trouble finding their food, but the bees with magnets lost their sense of direction.

Birds also use the sun's position as a guide to help them fly in the right direction when they migrate. But on cloudy days, the birds seem to use their

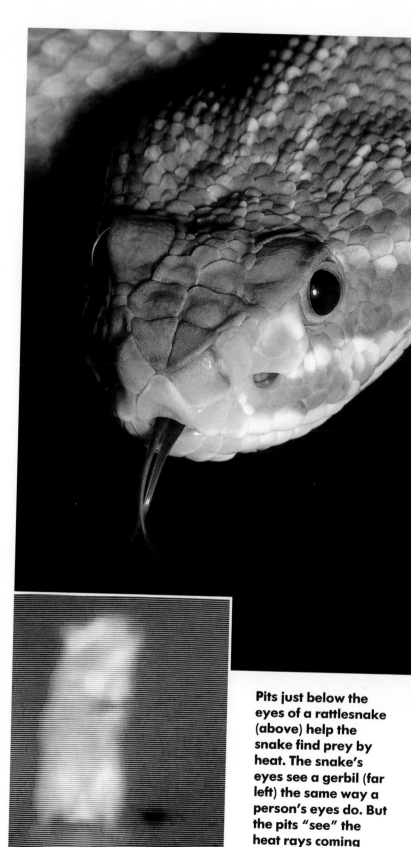

Pits just below the eyes of a rattlesnake (above) help the snake find prey by heat. The snake's eyes see a gerbil (far left) the same way a person's eyes do. But the pits "see" the heat rays coming from the gerbil's body (left).

natural compasses as a backup navigation system.

Monarch butterflies probably use their magnetic sense to find their way when they migrate, too. Monarchs journey up to 2,500 miles between their summer and winter homes in North America. Like birds, the monarchs seem to follow the sun. But because monarchs' bodies contain large amounts of magnetite, scientists think that the butterflies also follow the earth's magnetic field.

In some places the magnetic field changes to line up with faults in the earth's crust. One whale expert described these magnetic lines as highways on the ocean floor. Whales follow

these roads when they migrate. Whales also lose their way when the magnetic field changes. This may explain why they sometimes strand themselves on beaches.

PREDICTING THE FUTURE

Although all super senses have a natural explanation, people don't always know what that explanation is. Look at animals and earthquakes, for example.

The year was 1835. The place was the town of Concepcion, a seaport in southern Chile. A British admiral, Robert Fitzroy, describes what happened: "Towards ten o'clock in the morning screaming swarms of sea birds darkened the sky. At 11:30 the dogs fled out of the houses. Ten minutes later an earthquake destroyed the town." Was this a coincidence, or do animals really know when an earthquake is going to hit?

People have asked this question for thousands of years. The ancient Incas of South America believed the answer was *yes.* They kept catfish in ponds so they could watch them. If the catfish became restless, the people braced for an earthquake.

The Chinese have kept records for at least 3,000 years trying to match periods of unusual animal activity with earthquakes. Sometimes the two go together quite well. In the winter of 1974-75, the people of Haicheng noticed that farm animals in the area were getting jittery. Then snakes left their hibernation holes, even though the weather was icy. To the people of the city, the conclusion seemed obvious: earthquake!

Officials ordered everyone to leave the city and, just as the people thought, an earthquake struck. Fortunately, almost everyone had reached safety outside the city.

Why do animals act strangely before some earthquakes but not before others? No one knows. When animals do get restless and do things out of the ordinary, what causes their odd behavior? Again, no one knows.

The Chinese success in Haicheng may have been only what one news report called "guesswork and luck." According to a later account, the Chinese earthquake experts "issued at least ten false alarms for every successful prediction." Scientists agree that *sometimes* animals do strange things before earthquakes, but the age of reliable living earthquake predictors is not yet here.

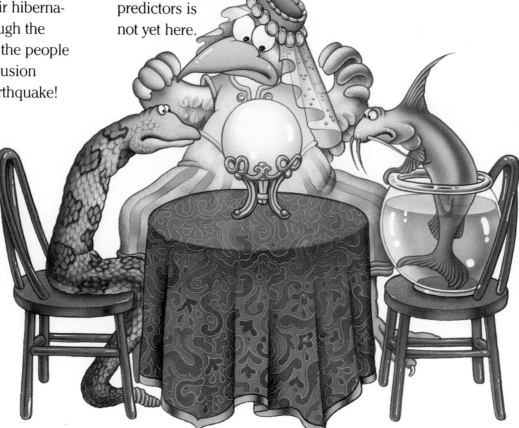

Credits

Cover, chapter openers, and all other art illustrations are by Jean Pidgeon.

Page 5: P.N. Raven/Planet Earth Pictures.

LOOK! LOOK!

8 top: Dave Fleetham/Tom Stack & Assoc. **bottom:** both by Dwight R. Kuhn. **9:** Gary Milburn/Tom Stack & Assoc. **10:** Rod Planck/M.L. Dembinsky Jr. Photography Assoc. **11 top:** Rod Planck/M.L. Dembinsky Jr. Photography Assoc. **bottom:** Anthony Bannister Photo Library. **12 top:** Larry Lipsky/DRK Photo. **bottom:** Scott L. Pearson. **13 top:** J. Carmichael Jr./NHPA. **bottom:** Russ Kinne/Comstock. **14 top:** Jane Burton/Bruce Coleman Ltd. **14-15:** S.L. Craig/Bruce Coleman Inc. **15 top:** Alan and Sandy Carey. **16 left:** Joe McDonald. **right:** Zig Leczczynski/Animals Animals. **17:** David Maitland/Planet Earth Pictures. **18:** Joe McDonald. **19:** Brian Parker/Tom Stack & Assoc. **20 top:** Robert Simpson. **bottom:** both by Robert L. Dunne. **22:** Patti Murray/Animals Animals. **23 top:** Charles Krebs. **bottom:** both by Terry Domico/Earth Images. **24:** Michael Fogden/DRK Photo. **25 top:** Michael Fogden/Oxford Scientific Films. **bottom:** Michael Fogden/DRK Photo. **26 top:** George W. Cox. **bottom:** Frans Lanting/Minden Pictures. **27:** George W. Cox. **28:** both by Edward S. Ross. **28-29:** Kenneth Lucas/Planet Earth Pictures.

NOISES, NOISES EVERYWHERE

32: Andrew Neal/Planet Earth Pictures. **33:** Joe McDonald. **34 top left:** Russ Kinne/Comstock. **top right:** Robert and Linda Mitchell. **bottom:** Alfred B. Thomas/Animals Animals. **35:** Jean-Paul Ferrero/Auscape. **36 left:** Sharon Cummings/M.L. Dembinsky Jr. Photography Assoc. **right:** Stan Osolinski/M.L. Dembinsky Jr. Photography Assoc. **37:** both by P.N. Raven/Planet Earth Pictures. **38-39:** Michael Fogden/Bruce Coleman Ltd. **40 top:** Stephen Dalton/Oxford Scientific Films. **bottom:** Merlin Tuttle/Bat Conservation International. **41:** Bob Talbot. **42:** both by C. Allen Morgan. **43:** Tom and Pat Leeson. **44:** Tom Edwards. **45:** Lynn Rodgers. **46 top:** Charles Krebs. **bottom:** G.I. Bernard/Oxford Scientific Films.

THE NOSE KNOWS

50: Akira Uchiyama. **50-51:** Frank S. Balthis. **52:** Doug Perrine/DRK Photo. **53 top:** Francisco Erize/Bruce Coleman Ltd. **bottom:** Michael Fogden/DRK Photo. **54:** both by Marty Snyderman. **55:** Rod Williams/Bruce Coleman Ltd. **56:** Marty Cordano/DRK Photo. **56-57:** Peter Pickford/NHPA. **57:** both by Edward S. Ross. **58 top:** Marty Stouffer Productions/Animals Animals. **bottom:** Gilbert van Ryckevorsel/Planet Earth Pictures. **59 top:** Kevin Shafer/Peter Arnold. **bottom:** Kennan Ward. **60:** Tom Walker. **61 left:** Jonathan Scott/Planet Earth Pictures. **right:** Anthony Bannister Photo Library. **62:** George Lepp/Comstock. **62-63:** Fred Bruemmer. **64-65:** Skip Moody/M.L. Dembinsky Jr. Photography Assoc. **66-67:** John Cooke/Oxford Scientific Films. **67:** R. Andrew Odum/Peter Arnold. **68 left top:** John Chellman/Animals Animals. **left bottom:** Kim Taylor/Bruce Coleman Ltd. **right:** Erwin and Peggy Bauer. **69:** C.B. Frith/Bruce Coleman Ltd.

KEEPING IN TOUCH

72-73: Dwight R. Kuhn. **73 top:** Patti Murray/Animals Animals. **bottom:** Tom McHugh/Photo Researchers. **74:** Mark I. Jones. **75 top:** Anthony Bannister Photo Library. **bottom:** Jeff Foott/DRK Photo. **76 top:** Norbert Wu. **bottom:** Susan Blanchet/M.L. Dembinsky Jr. Photography Assoc. **77:** Linda Pitkin/Planet Earth Pictures. **78:** Dwight R. Kuhn. **79:** Dwight R. Kuhn. **80-81:** Rudie Kuiter/Oxford Scientific Films. **81:** John McGregor/Peter Arnold. **82:** Doug Perrine. **83 top:** Jean-Paul Ferrero/Auscape. **bottom:** Gunter Ziesler. **85:** both by Jane Burton/Bruce Coleman Ltd.

SUPER SENSES

88: Dave Fleetham/Tom Stack & Assoc. **89 top:** Dave Watts/Tom Stack & Assoc. **90:** Gunter Ziesler/Peter Arnold. **91 bottom left:** Anthony Bannister Photo Library. **bottom right:** S.L. Craig Jr./Bruce Coleman Inc. **top:** Michael Dick/Animals Animals. **92:** Stan Osolinsky/M.L. Dembinsky Jr. Photography Assoc.

Library of Congress Cataloging-in-Publication Data

What do animals see, hear, smell, and feel?

"Ranger Rick books."
Includes index.
Summary: Explores how animal senses are often superior to those of people.
1. Senses and sensation—Juvenile literature. 2. Animals—Physiology—Juvenile literature. [1. Senses and sensation. 2. Animals] I. National Wildlife Federation.

QP434.W45 1990
591.1'82 90-6171

ISNB 0-945051-23-9
ISBN 0-945051-24-7 (lib. bdg.)

Index

95

Working for the Nature of Tomorrow®
NATIONAL WILDLIFE FEDERATION
1400 Sixteenth Street, N.W., Washington, D.C. 20036-2266